Financial Crisis

What to Do When the Bottom
Drops Out

Jim Newheiser

New
Growth
Press

newgrowthpress.com

New Growth Press, Greensboro, NC 27404
newgrowthpress.com
Copyright © 2020 by Jim Newheiser

Scripture quotations are taken from the NEW AMERICAN
STANDARD BIBLE®, Copyright © 1960, 1962, 1963,
1968, 1971, 1972, 1973, 1975, 1977, 1995 by The Lockman
Foundation. Used by permission.

Cover Design: Tom Temple
Interior Design and Typesetting: Gretchen Logterman

ISBN: 978-1-64507-126-6 (Print)
ISBN: 978-1-64507-127-3 (eBook)

Library of Congress Cataloging-in-Publication Data

Names: Newheiser, Jim, author.
Title: Financial crisis : what to do when the bottom drops out / by Jim
  Newheiser.
Description: Greensboro, NC : New Growth Press, 2020. | Includes
  bibliographical references. | Summary: "Counselor and author Jim
  Newheiser takes us through the timeless wisdom and comfort of God's
  Word
  to help us face frightening financial storms"-- Provided by publisher.
Identifiers: LCCN 2020030362 (print) | LCCN 2020030363 (ebook) | ISBN
  9781645071266 (print) | ISBN 9781645071273 (ebook)
Subjects: LCSH: Finance, Personal--Religious aspects--Christianity.
Classification: LCC HG179 .N4484 2020 (print) | LCC HG179 (ebook) | DDC
  332.024--dc23
LC record available at https://lccn.loc.gov/2020030362
LC ebook record available at https://lccn.loc.gov/2020030363

Printed in India

27 26 25 24 23 22 21 20   1 2 3 4 5

Roger thought that he had finally gotten his financial affairs in order. He has a steady income, has recently refinanced his substantial student debt, and has almost entirely eliminated his credit card debt. As he is working on his taxes, he anticipates how he and his wife, Jessica, could enjoy their refund. Perhaps this year they could finally go on a cruise. But then Roger received a call from his tax preparer saying that Roger had failed to pay sufficient estimated taxes and owes the IRS $15,000. Roger is stunned. He has no idea how he can come up with that kind of money.

John has been growing beets on his family farm in Montana for fifteen years. Last year there was a drought, so he barely broke even. He had to borrow money from the bank in order to plant this season's crop. This summer's precipitation had been sufficient and it looked like John was going to have a bumper crop. Then just before harvest time, a week of torrential rains completely flooded the fields, preventing him from moving his machinery onto the property. By the time the floodwaters receded, the crops were rotting and worthless. John is fearful that he may lose his farm if he can't pay back his bank loan.

Jane and Pete have been married for forty years, during which they have lived frugally and have faithfully saved. They eagerly anticipated retirement, when they planned to move closer to their children and grandchildren. Two weeks after Jane and Pete gave their employers notice of their plans to retire, the stock market suddenly crashed, losing over 30 percent of its value. Jane and Pete's financial advisor has told them that they can no longer afford to retire this year. With the economy in the tank,

Pete isn't sure he will be able to keep his job, and Jane has already been told that her employer isn't willing to let her withdraw her offer to retire.

In the late 1920s, my grandfather was in college studying agriculture and was anticipating graduation, marrying his sweetheart, and joining the family's ranching business in south Texas. Sadly, just as he was about to graduate, the country entered into the Great Depression and there was no job available for him in the family business. Turns out he wasn't ready for a Depression.

Sam owns a popular local gym in a suburb of Charlotte, North Carolina. He was a follower of Dave Ramsey's radio program about finances and had been very careful to avoid debt and to have three months of emergency savings on hand. But when the COVID-19 pandemic hit, all the gyms in the state were shut down. During the first three months Sam burned through all of his emergency savings. He was able to get a government grant, but as the lockdown continued into the fifth month Sam wasn't receiving any income from clients and both his mortgage and the rent on his facility were past due. He thought he was prepared for a crisis, but it turns out that he wasn't ready for a pandemic.

People face many different types of financial crises—many of them completely unanticipated. While some face this hardship due to poor financial management or other preventable factors, many face financial crisis due to unforeseen and unavoidable circumstances (economic downturn, health complications, pandemics, etc.).

God is not unaware of our financial difficulties and he knows our needs. His Word contains timeless wisdom and comfort to help us to face frightening financial storms. Psalm 19:7 reminds us, "The law of the LORD is perfect, restoring the soul; The testimony of the LORD is sure, making wise the simple." Scripture teaches us both how to prepare for financial crises and how to face a crisis when it comes. The Bible also teaches us to put our ultimate trust in God and not in our riches: "He who trusts in his riches will fall, but the righteous will flourish like the green leaf" (Proverbs 11:28).

Preparing for a Financial Crisis

In this life, there will be financial hardships and troubles to navigate. One result of the fall is that our work is under the curse (Genesis 3:17–19). As we try to eke out a living, proverbial thorns and thistles are to be expected. Throughout human history there have been wars, financial recessions and depressions, pandemics, famine, and drought. It seems that when nations and individuals think that they are secure, the Lord often humbles them with a crisis (Daniel 4). Ongoing prosperity, security, and stability will not occur until Jesus returns and establishes his perfect kingdom.

While we cannot entirely avoid unexpected financial calamity, we can seek to be ready for this difficulty when it inevitably comes. When the Lord revealed to Pharaoh in a dream that a great famine was coming, Joseph wisely helped Egypt to be prepared for the crisis by saving food during the years of prosperity (Genesis 41).[1] Unlike Joseph, we don't know when the next crisis is coming. But since we do know that financially lean times are inevitable, it's wise to prepare. In Pharaoh's dream there were seven healthy cows (representing the times of prosperity) who were then consumed by seven thin cows (representing years of famine). This illustration helps us see the need to act wisely during our prosperous years, knowing that years of scarcity are likely to cycle around in the future. Here are some helpful ways to prepare for financial challenges (which are also helpful strategies when you are facing a crisis).

1. Create and keep a budget. "The plans of the diligent lead surely to advantage, but everyone who is hasty comes surely to poverty," Proverbs 21:5 reminds us. A budget is a plan for how you will spend and save your money. A wise goal would be for your income to surpass your expenditures, which will help provide a surplus for savings. It will also anticipate periodic future financial outlays (taxes, insurance, car repairs and replacement, etc.). In order for your budget to work, it must be implemented as you keep records to ensure that you remain within your spending plan. There are many online tools that can help you to do this easily and effectively. One recommended by the *Wall Street Journal* is mint.com. Crown Ministries also has some useful financial tools on their website (www.crown.org).

2. Limit your lifestyle. Proverbs 21:17 observes, "He who loves pleasure will become a poor man; he who loves wine and oil will not become rich." During seasons of prosperity, it can be tempting to fully enjoy the fruits of our labor, with little thought of the future. We can afford the latest model phones and luxurious vacations, so we indulge. We don't worry about the cost of frequently dining out and buying expensive coffee every day. Times are good.

3. Avoid debt. It is true that "the borrower becomes the lender's slave" (Proverbs 22:7). Debt can be a great temptation. It allows us to live beyond our present income and lets us enjoy possessions and experiences without having to wait to accumulate the money to pay for them. While we can't say that it is always wrong to borrow money (i.e., a mortgage), we should be very careful about taking on debt. Rather than stretching financially to buy a dream house, it might be wiser to purchase a more modest home with a more manageable payment, which we could continue to afford in an economic downturn (Proverbs 24:27). Rather than borrowing to buy a high-end late model vehicle, it is usually wiser to save for a more basic car for which you can pay in cash. A general rule is never to owe more on anything than the amount for which you could sell it in a crisis. Credit card debt is especially dangerous because it typically is accumulated through failure to live by a budget, and its interest rates are very high. Student loans should be minimized, or avoided if possible, especially when the education or training is not likely to result in a well-paying job. Such loans often place a family under a very heavy debt burden for a long period of time. Many are able to minimize student debt through taking courses at a local community college or by paying for their education through military service.[2]

Sooner or later, steep debt becomes an enslaving burden. Those with the most debt typically suffer much more during a financial crisis. Consequences of excessive debt can include home foreclosure and personal or business bankruptcy. Proverbs vividly warns of the consequences of taking on debt. Proverbs 22:27 reminds us, "If you have nothing with which to pay, why should he take your bed from under you?" I also love the profound quote by the often-troubled character Wilkens Micawber in the Charles Dickens classic, *David Copperfield*. "Annual income twenty pounds, annual expenditure nineteen pounds nineteen and six, result happiness. Annual income twenty pounds, annual expenditure twenty pounds nought and six, result misery."[3]

4. *Save*. The key to Egypt and its neighbors surviving the lengthy famine in Joseph's day was saving and storing up food by restraining themselves from consuming all of the abundance of the "fat cow" years. Even the ant saves for the future as she "prepares her food in the summer and gathers her provision in the harvest" (Proverbs 6:8). We also do wisely to save for troubled times. Conventional wisdom is that a family should have three to six months' worth of expenses saved in order to survive a financial crisis. This practice requires self-discipline during times of prosperity. Businesses and families who enter a financial crisis with savings often not only survive but prosper through hard times. Pharaoh, after following Joseph's advice to save grain during the "fat cow" years, was able to greatly increase his wealth by selling his excess to people from other nations and through buying up land in Egypt.

"The people of all the earth came to Egypt to buy grain from Joseph, because the famine was severe in all the earth. . . . So Joseph bought all the land of Egypt for Pharaoh, for every Egyptian sold his field, because the famine was severe upon them. Thus the land became Pharaoh's" (Genesis 41:57; 47:20).[4] Those with savings and without debt often come out ahead in times of economic crisis.

5. Maintain and upgrade your marketable skills. Proverbs 22:29 observes the wider range of employment options available to highly skilled workers: "Do you see a man skilled in his work? He will stand before kings; he will not stand before obscure men." During times of prosperity, unemployment is often low and it is relatively easy to find a job. But during an economic crisis with high unemployment, often only the most skilled workers will be able to find gainful employment. It is wise to take courses to upgrade your present skills, or even to acquire additional skills which might be useful during hard times. Some people are too dependent upon their present job. They are unprepared for the possibility of their employer falling onto hard times or deciding that their services are no longer needed. If this were to happen, do you have skills by which you could get another job?

6. Build strong ties with your church community. The early church was characterized by sacrificial generosity toward those in need (Acts 2:44–45; 4:32–37; Galatians 2:10). During the first century, the Lord used a financial crisis (famine) to unite the church as the Gentile churches helped the Jewish churches (Acts 11:28–30; 2 Corinthians 8–9). We should be generous to the needs of our church family as God prospers us (1 Corinthians 16:1–2; Ephesians 4:28). And as members of the church, we should be prepared to care for those who are in economic distress.

7. *Trust God, not your wealth.* While it is wise to plan and to be prepared for a financial crisis, our ultimate trust cannot be in our savings or our preparation. Our careful planning is still subject to God's sovereign will. Proverbs 16:19 reminds us, "The mind of a man plans his way, but the LORD directs his steps." We must plan and prepare humbly, remembering we are not in control.

Even as we wisely prepare for a financial downturn, we need to remember that no matter how much financial wealth we accumulate, we cannot take it with us into the next life. The parable of the rich fool, whose riches were worthless when he faced death, powerfully illustrates this point (see Luke 12:16–21). Our confidence needs to be rooted deeply in the Lord and his provision, remembering that earthly treasure will not last (Matthew 6:19–20). Instead of an over-preoccupation with material concerns, we are to pour ourselves into investment into the kingdom of God (Matthew 6:33).

Facing a Financial Crisis

Perhaps at this point a financial crisis has already met you head-on, and you do not have the ability to go back in time to put some of these preparatory measures in place. What can you do now?

First, turn to the Lord in your distress. Whether this hardship has come through poor planning or it has landed on your doorstep due to no fault of yours, your heavenly Father cares about everything that concerns you, and he stands ready to walk you through this trial. Here are some specific pointers for seeking him during this time:

1. Cry out to God for help. During times of plenty we may repeat the Lord's Prayer, "Give us this day our daily bread" (Matthew 6:11) with little serious thought. But when we aren't sure how we will be able to pay for this month's food and housing, we express our dependence upon God's provision with much greater fervency. Ask him to help you to find work so that you can provide for your family. Ask him to help you to make wise financial decisions. Ask for the gift of faith so that you can trust him during this hard time.

2. Examine your own heart. God may use a financial crisis to expose areas of sin or to loosen your grip on earthly riches and to value heavenly treasure (Matthew 6:19–21). What might the Lord be teaching you during this time? The psalmist prays, "Search me, O God, and know my heart; Try me and know my anxious thoughts; and see if there be any hurtful way in me, and lead me in the everlasting way" (Psalm 139:23–24). What can this wilderness season teach us about what is in our hearts? As we seek the Lord in our time of trial, perhaps we will discover that our trust has been in our own resources rather than in him. Or perhaps this lean season will help us realize we've been chasing the wrong treasure.

3. Confess your failings. If your financial mess is largely of your own making, rather than creating excuses or complaining about your bad luck, repent of your sins of overspending, taking on too much debt, covetousness, or presumption toward him (1 John 1:8–9). Jesus has made a way for us to be forgiven for all of our sins. Go to him and confess everything. You will find that the Lord is forgiving, merciful, and compassionate toward his children, especially as we approach him humbly. Psalm 103:8, 10–14 paints a beautiful picture of the tenderness of our God when we come to him for mercy:

> The Lord is compassionate and gracious, slow to anger and abounding in lovingkindness. . . . He has not dealt with us according to our sins, nor rewarded us according to our iniquities. For as high as the heavens are above the earth, so great is His lovingkindess toward those who fear Him. As far as the east is from the west, so far has He removed our transgressions from us. Just as a father has compassion on his children, so the Lord has compassion on those who fear Him. For He Himself knows our frame; He is mindful that we are but dust.

4. Trust God to meet your needs. You can rest knowing the Lord's attention to your needs. The psalmist declares, "I have been young and now I am old, yet I have not seen the righteous forsaken or his descendants begging bread" (Psalm 37:25). Jesus exhorts us to remember God's loving commitment to our provision in Matthew 6:31–32: "Do not worry then, saying 'What will we eat?' or 'What will we drink?' or 'What will we wear for clothing?' For the Gentiles eagerly seek all these things; for your heavenly Father knows that you need all these things." In the midst of a crisis we need not be consumed with fear and worry because our ultimate hope is not in our politicians, employers, or even ourselves. Our hope is fixed upon our heavenly Father who loves us and will provide what we need. Take heart in remembering God's ultimate display of his love and care for you by sending Jesus: "What then shall we say to these things? If God is for us, who is against us? He who did not spare his own Son, but delivered him over for us all, how will he not also with him freely give us all things?" (Romans 8:31–32). In the midst of a crisis, Christians can stand out as those who are not consumed by fear as they put their hope and trust in the Lord.

In addition to turning to God in confession, prayer, and faith, we are also responsible to take wise action to fulfill our financial obligations. Trusting God doesn't mean that we are passive. Here are some suggestions to help you thoughtfully approach this lean season:

1. Radically reduce expenses. My mother, who lived through much of the Great Depression and all of World

War II, tells stories of how her family lived frugally and how the entire nation had to endure the rationing of essential items. Just as a nation must take dramatic steps to survive during calamity, a family must also be prepared to slash its budget down to the bare minimum in order to come through a financial crisis. Paul challenges us, "If we have food and covering, with these we shall be content" (1 Timothy 6:8). Be prepared to look at every bill and every dollar you are spending as you reduce expenses to absolute necessities. This may include eliminating cable or digital streaming entertainment, or even downsizing your housing or reducing the number of cars you own. For some of us, lifestyle reduction can be very hard. One benefit is that we may learn that ultimate satisfaction comes from the Lord and that earthly pleasures are fleeting (Isaiah 55:1–2).

2. Find ways to increase income. The job market often changes in the midst of a widespread financial crisis. You may need to find a different kind of employment. Where are people finding work in the new economy? For example, during the COVID-19 pandemic while millions were losing their jobs, many found employment through working as delivery drivers, grocers, and even temperature checkers. Don't be too proud to take a job that might seem beneath your skills and experience. Your worth is not defined by what you do—it's defined by being a child of God. Use the internet and your network of friends who might know of job leads. You may need to consider a longer commute or even relocating if you can't find a job locally.

If you don't have a job, your full-time role is to keep looking for work (Ecclesiastes 11:6).

Seeking employment during an economic downturn can be very discouraging if you experience many rejections. Just as the widows Ruth and Naomi depended upon God's help, which came through the provision of the faithful redeemer Boaz (Ruth 2), pray that God will help you by providing gainful employment. Also pray that he will help you not to lose heart.

As you continue to think creatively about new streams of revenue during difficult times, one option may be to rent out an extra room in your house. This would require logistical adjustments in your household but you could look for someone you already know and trust who is also seeking to reduce their living expenses. Another idea would be to sell items in your home you are not currently using, such as musical instruments or extra furniture.

3. Negotiate with your creditors. If you find yourself overextended and unable to make full payments on your debts, you are free, in good faith, to see if more favorable terms can be agreed upon which would enable you to keep making payments and would keep them from having to write off a bad debt. Proverbs encourages a person who has taken on an onerous financial debt to negotiate for relief: "If you have been snared with the words of your mouth, have been caught with the words of your mouth, do this then, my son, and deliver yourself; since you have come into the hand of your neighbor, go humble yourself, and importune your neighbor. . . . Deliver yourself like a gazelle from the hunter's hand and like a bird from the hand of the fowler" (Proverbs 6:2–3, 5).

4. Be ready to help others who are worse off than you. Our first obligation is to our families, especially our elderly or widowed parents. Paul teaches, "But if anyone does not provide for his own, and especially for those of his household, he has denied the faith and is worse than an unbeliever" (1 Timothy 5:8). We also are to be concerned with the needs of our brothers and sisters in Christ. Paul commends the believers in Macedonia whose own dire economic circumstances did not stop them from helping believers who were worse off in Judea during the famine in the first century: "in a great ordeal of affliction their abundance of joy and their deep poverty overflowed in the wealth of their liberality. For I testify that according to their ability, and beyond their ability, they gave of their own accord" (2 Corinthians 8:2–3). As we become aware of needs and hardships among our fellow believers, we should prayerfully consider how we can emulate the early church by opening our wallets and even our homes to brothers and sisters who are in desperate need. We also consider giving generously to various ministries including our local church which might experience greater need during times of economic crisis. Look around at your community as well. Consider how you and your family might help others more needy than yourselves—there have been lots of opportunities in our community to volunteer to bring food to the elderly and shut-ins (Galatians 6:10).

Facing Hard Questions in an Economic Crisis

During times of financial disaster, many hard questions can arise.

Is a Christian allowed to walk away from his debts? The psalmist declares, "The wicked borrows and does not pay back" (Psalm 37:21). The book of Proverbs also exhorts us to faithfully pay our debts, whenever we are able: "Do not withhold good from those to whom it is due, when it is in your power to do it. Do not say to your neighbor, 'Go and come back, and tomorrow I will give it,' when you have it with you" (Proverbs 3:27–28). A faithful Christian will do everything in his or her power to meet their financial obligations and will not try to use the law to circumvent their responsibilities. For example, if due to a crash in the real estate market one owes more on their home than it is worth, they should, if able, continue to make their payments—even if others are walking away from their "upside down" mortgages. The godly person keeps his promises even when it is costly: "He swears to his own hurt and does not change" (Psalm 15:4).

Should we borrow money to try to pay our debts? NO! When spending exceeds income, many families are tempted to use high interest credit card debt and other forms of credit to weather the financial storm. This approach can tempt people to delay the radical steps of cost-cutting and income-seeking which can directly address the problem. Almost inevitably, the result of borrowing more to pay down other debts will be that the family will have dug themselves into a deeper pit of debt from which it will be almost impossible to emerge.

When, if ever, may a Christian enter into bankruptcy or foreclosure? Some people find themselves forced into bankruptcy or foreclosure, not because they are trying to escape their obligations, but because they simply can't come close to meeting their financial obligations due to circumstances beyond their control—typically due to a dramatic loss of income. If the borrower has been guilty of unwisely overextending themselves, they should seek God's forgiveness, and, where appropriate, they should apologize to the lender (especially if a friend or a family member is involved). Some Christians, after bankruptcy, have decided that their obligations go beyond their legal obligations, and have, when prosperity returns, gone back to their lenders and repaid loans which had been voided by bankruptcy courts.

Should a Christian who is in the midst of a financial crisis continue to give to the church? If one has massive debts and is likely to go into bankruptcy, then to give large sums to the church could, in effect, be stealing from lenders to whom their money is owed. On the other hand, a family in the midst of a financial crisis may wisely choose to make room in their radically diminished budget to give to the Lord's work. The smaller financial gifts they are now able to give may be more sacrificial than the larger sums they donated during the years of prosperity.

When is it right to accept help from others? Paul warns that those who are unwilling to work should not be helped by the church: "For even when we were with you, we used to give this order: if anyone is not willing to work, then he is not to eat, either" (2 Thessalonians 3:10). But if you are doing everything in your power to find work and to reduce expenses and still have need, then it is not wrong to receive economic help from family, from the church, and from government programs. It would be wrong, however, to become dependent upon such assistance to the extent that you stop trying to find a way to provide for yourself and hope to have some left over by which you can help others (Ephesians 4:28).

Final Considerations

As you face the storm of financial crisis, remember that God is sovereign. Just as the Egyptian famine in Joseph's day was ordained by God for his own good purposes, we should always remember that the financial hardships we face do not come upon us, our nation, or the entire world by chance. God is in control. He is working out his own good and just purposes. Psalm 115:3 reminds us, "But our God is in the heavens; He does whatever He pleases." We also can trust that his plan is the best possible plan and will ultimately work out for our good (Romans 8:28).

God did not promise us sustained prosperity and stability in this life. Perhaps one of the benefits of a large-scale economic crisis is that it should silence, or at least discredit, false teachers who claim that with enough faith every Christian can always be rich, happy, and healthy in this age. Our Savior was "a man of sorrows and acquainted with grief" (Isaiah 53:3) who possessed almost no earthly wealth (Luke 9:58). While many of the heroes of the faith described in Scripture experienced victory and success, others who were equally faithful suffered hardship in this life and they are praised as "men of whom the world was not worthy" (Hebrews 11:38). The righteous prophets often had to suffer God's judgment upon their wicked nation, even though they were not at fault (i.e., Jeremiah and Habakkuk). We too may suffer along with the rest of our communities or even the entire world as the general effects of sin are experienced, or as the Lord sees fit to bring particular judgments.

Our place of everlasting peace and prosperity is in the world to come. Your best life will come later. The hope of the faithful saints of the past was the city of God which was yet to come (Hebrews 11:10). Paul reminds us, "our citizenship is in heaven from which also we eagerly wait for a Savior, the Lord Jesus Christ" (Philippians 3:20). In light of this we should invest our time, treasure, and talents in the kingdom which is yet to come: "Do not store up for yourselves treasures on earth, where moth and rust destroy, and where thieves break in and steal. But store up for yourselves treasures in heaven, where neither moth nor rust destroys, and where thieves do not break in or steal" (Matthew 6:19–20). While we can legitimately and thankfully enjoy God's blessings in this life (1 Timothy 4:3–4), our great hope and treasure is in the life to come.

Remember that our greatest treasure is Christ. We have a Savior who willingly entered into our fallen world to pay the spiritual debts we incurred through our sin and to enrich us with his perfect righteousness. Second Corinthians 8:9 reminds us, "For you know the grace of our Lord Jesus Christ, that though He was rich, yet for your sake He became poor, so that you through His poverty might become rich." If God has shown you mercy by forgiving your sins for Jesus's sake and incorporating you into his glorious kingdom, you are rich indeed!

Endnotes

1. Acts 11:27–30 offers another example of preparation for a crisis as the early church prepared for a worldwide famine.

2. Businesses and governments also are lured by the temptation of debt. Companies often seek to expand the size of their business through risky borrowing. Governments, through debt, can offer more benefits without increasing taxation.

3. Charles Dickens, *David Copperfield* (London, Edinburgh, New York: Thomas Nelson and Sons, 1906), 184. First Published 1850.

4. This is not to say that Pharaoh's practice of taking people's land was commendable or biblical, but this story serves to illustrate that his principle of saving for future hardships was wise.